Manifesting Alignment

Secrets to Becoming a Vibrational Match to Your Desires

Law of Attraction Short Reads, Book 10

Copyright Elena G. Rivers © 2022

All rights reserved. No part of this publication may be reproduced, stored in a retrieval system, or transmitted, in any form or by any means, electronic, mechanical, photocopying, recording, or otherwise, without the author and the publishers' prior written permission.

The scanning, uploading, and distributing this book via the Internet or any other means without the author's permission are illegal and punishable by law. Please purchase only authorized electronic editions and do not participate in or encourage electronic piracy of copyrighted materials.

Elena G. Rivers © Copyright 2022 - All rights reserved.

ISBN: 978-1-80095-080-1

Legal Notice:

This book is copyright protected—it for personal use only.

Disclaimer Notice:

Please note that the information contained in this book is for inspirational and entertainment purposes only. Every attempt has been made to provide accurate, up-to-date, and completely reliable information. No warranties of any kind are expressed or implied. Readers acknowledge that the author is not engaging in the rendering of legal, financial, health, medical, or professional advice. By reading this book, the reader agrees that under no circumstances are we responsible for any losses, direct or indirect, which are incurred due to the use of the information contained within this book, including, but not limited to, errors, omissions, or inaccuracies. The information provided in this book is for entertainment purposes only. If you are struggling with serious problems, including chronic illness, mental instability, or legal issues, please consult with your local registered health care or legal professional as soon as possible. This book is not a substitute for professional or legal advice.

Contents

Introduction – Fusing Yourself with Your Desires and Reaching Joyful Manifesting States 7

Secret #1 Audit Your Deep-Rooted Beliefs 34

Secret #2 Activate Your Inner Leadership 46

Secret #3 The Power of Letting Go and LOA Detox (Feel Good Just to Feel Good) 66

Conclusion – A Few More Vibrational Tricks to Boost Your Manifesting Powers 77

Join Our Manifestation Newsletter and Get a Free eBook 89

Introduction – Fusing Yourself with Your Desires and Reaching Joyful Manifesting States

Dear Reader and Ambitious Spiritual Seeker! It's time to fuse yourself with your desires. You, too, can experience the joys of becoming one with your dream reality...

There's no anxiety, shame, guilt, or doubt when you are in this pure, heart-based state. There's only peace, harmony, joy, and love...

I'm so excited to be guiding you on this journey of unlimited empowerment to help you explore your full potential!

I'm writing this book with two reader avatars in mind: those new to the Law of Attraction/manifestation and seasoned spiritual and manifestation explorers. I believe there are no "levels" here in the metaphysical world. So, I see no reason to label my content as for "beginners" or "advanced practitioners" anymore. We are all both beginners and advanced at the same time!

Because this journey is that of a non-stop exploration and discovery. So, we are continually advancing while discovering something new – and now I create and structure my books from this mindset (and heartset).

So, if your mind starts to wander and think thoughts such as: "Oh, but I'm new to this material, will this work for me if I've never studied LOA before?" or: "Will I find something new here? Come on!!! There's nothing new here. I already know this…"

Please send it on a well-deserved holiday!

It's time to start learning with our hearts and release the shackles of our minds. As weird as it may sound, our minds often hold us back.

One of the most fundamental concepts of LOA is being mindful of your thoughts and staying positive. This will be so much easier to practice if you start releasing any current beliefs and expectations you may have around studying manifestation and spirituality (such as, for example, organizing books and materials into "levels").

I believe that the task I'm giving you now, the simple task of reading this book with your heart, more than with your mind, will speed up your positive manifestations. It will also help you feel good and release the negative mind chatter – one of the most giant manifesting blocks!

So, once again, you can send your mind on a holiday as you read this book with your heart! Oh, and there's no "correct order." I organized different concepts you can practice as "vibrational secrets." Tune into your heart and intuition to focus on the ones that truly resonate with you at this stage of your journey!

The energetic principles and techniques I share with you in this book come from years of my personal experimentation and manifestation practice. Over the years, I transformed many obstacles into opportunities while substituting fear for faith.

I promised myself to stay on this journey forever. For me, there's no beginning and no end. Staying on the journey of conscious, heart-based manifesting is one of the greatest desires I could ever manifest because most of my days feel like magic. And I'm only getting started!

Now, I use my energy and creativity to transfer the concepts and teachings that have helped me transform so that you, too, can experience the joys of manifesting lifestyle!

Yes, because to me, it's a lifestyle! As I said, there's no beginning and no end. I love to manifest. I live to manifest. And because I consciously manifest, I can live a truly magical life in alignment with my values and desires.

I desire to spread good vibes and joy with as many people as I can so that they, too, can share this knowledge with others.

But first, you need to embrace it and live it. You need to embody the manifestation teachings and principles so that you can be an inspiration to those who need it and help us raise the vibration of the planet.

By practicing and internalizing the secrets covered in this book, your mindset and energy will shift, and you will be amazed at what you can create!

While reading this book alone can help you raise your vibration and explore new levels of awareness, to create the best results and profound transformations, I highly recommend you give yourself some time and space to practice the concepts I share. Use daily situations and your regular tasks to practice what you learn.

And even if you feel like you've mastered something, there's always more you can explore. You can go deeper!

Of course, don't force yourself into anything; instead, get started with the tips that resonate with you. Because, if you feel attracted to them, it means that your heart and mind really need them!

Now, if you've been studying the Law of Attraction and manifestation, you already know how important it is to be a vibrational match to your desires. But the biggest hurdle that so many people on this journey face (and I've been there as well) is: *how to become a vibrational match to your desires? Is there a formula you could follow to manifest faster?*

And finally, the questions I used to ask myself when I first began this journey:

-Could it be that trying too hard to be a match for something pushes it away?

-How to reach clean, neutral, happy states to stop worrying about our desires?

-How to release negative beliefs or past conditioning to realize what we really want?

-Why complete alignment, that is- knowing what you want and having pure desires is so important?

Finally- why going after goals and desires that are not truly yours can only make things harder or add to manifesting unwanted circumstances?

It is my intention that after going through the contents of this book, you will realize the answers to these questions for yourself. One of the biggest manifestation blocks that so many of us experience is that we lose touch with our true, authentic selves and our natural desires.

Instead, we put on a society mask and succumb to either peer pressure or what we think is expected of us.

This is ego-based manifesting, and it can often get us on the path of misalignment. For example, you may find yourself working very hard doing something you strongly dislike, pursuing a goal that is not coming from your heart to impress people you don't even like or people who don't respect you. But, when you dive deeper, you realize you'd chosen a goal that wasn't even yours, just to seek validation or approval.

Now, if you've ever found yourself in a similar situation, don't worry, you're not alone, and there's no judgment. I've been there as well, and since my ego was very talented and stubborn (to say the least, haha!), it became a pattern for me. So, I spent years chasing something that wasn't even in proper alignment with what I really wanted.

Whatever you desire to manifest, the first step is to always dive deep and mindfully investigate the authenticity of your goal. One of the questions I always find very helpful is: "Does it feel light or heavy?".

If it feels heavy, chances are, you're desiring to manifest a goal that's not truly yours. And to succeed with this material, I recommend you use it the heart-based way! Focus on desires that are truly yours and come from your heart.

Another question that can help determine whether the goal you're working on is truly yours is:

Imagine you're very successful with your goal. You've manifested it and did very well. But most people will never know about your success; you can only share it with a few people, like your loved ones and people involved in manifesting your goal. Will you still want it?

If the answer is *yes*, it means you desire to manifest something for yourself and don't care about validation or approval from others. Of course, you can still get it; there's nothing wrong with that. However, your primary motivation that drives you to manifest your goal is truly yours and will make you very happy.

You're passionate about your goal and the process that leads to it. You will persist (in a forceless, joyful, and graceful way) until your goal is manifested and even after achieving it. In other words, your goal is a natural extension of you. You don't see any reason to stop. You just keep going!

Two people can have similar goals but different intentions.

For example, Barbara and Jane want to start their own YouTube channels.

Barbara wants to be a YouTuber because she wants fame and recognition. She wants to grow her subscribers as fast as possible just to be able to impress others with her online success.

She wants other people to validate her. She seeks instant fame and approval. So, the goal of manifesting a successful YouTube channel is not really hers. It's not coming from her heart. Yes, she can manifest some surface-level success and will most likely resort to some tactics she won't admit, such as buying fake subscribers. She might even burn out at some point.

The journey of manifesting success will be very hard and stressful for her. Negative comments will be a nightmare because, after all, she's doing the YouTube thing to impress others and always be right. Barbara often feels stuck or keeps jumping around different topics. She feels envious of others having success on YouTube and often copies them in hopes of having the same success, but most of the time, she feels disappointed.

Her energy and effort would be much better spent on changing her goals and choosing something she's truly passionate about while doing her own thing.

Jane starts her channel around the same time, but her mindset and energy are different. She's not in it to impress people with how many subscribers she can get and how fast she can grow. She's in it because...she wants to be a high-vibe, positivity-spreading YouTuber and help people with her videos.

She starts her channel about the topics she's passionate about and continually studies to fully internalize. She's patient and doesn't expect overnight success. Her journey is also her destination. She feels confident in herself and shows up authentically as herself.

Her intention is to share her knowledge and help other people. She also desires to attract soul-aligned subscribers, people who resonate with her message. So, she's not getting obsessed with the latest trends. And she doesn't pay much attention to how many subscribers she can get as fast as possible. Of course, she's pleased and grateful to see more and more people subscribe to her channel. But her main goal is to attract people who are ready for and will benefit from her teachings. Yes, she sees herself as a teacher who uses the YouTube platform to educate her students rather than a trend-chasing YouTuber. So, she focuses on authentic self-expression, one of her deepest desires.

She understands that getting an occasional hate comment from a troll is expected on this journey. She learns how to protect herself energetically and keeps doing her own thing. She doesn't get involved in hate conversations or try to prove someone wrong. Instead, she sends them love and light while staying focused on her loyal subscribers. She's mindful about how she interacts with her subscribers and doesn't treat them as a number to reach her goal and impress others.

Sure, her growth takes time. But it's steady and authentic. And after several years of aligned action and a heart-based mindset, she can manifest fantastic success on YouTube and receive massive compensation from different monetization avenues.

She also has a loyal fanbase and continuous opportunities for growth. She is famous in her field and has become an authority in her niche. Even though her original desire wasn't about receiving fame or recognition, and her focus was on sharing her message and being authentic, she now manifests what so many people desire – fame, money, and recognition.

These two stories teach us the importance of authenticity and following our goals in a love-based and heartful way. The manifestation example I used is related to what I like to call creative business, and these manifestations do require action. Preferably daily action. However, some manifestations don't need much action and can happen spontaneously, pretty much on autopilot as you energetically align with what you desire.

But of course, if your desire is to manifest success as a professional, businessperson, creative, social media influencer, actor, entertainer, athlete, etc., you will need to take consistent action to reach your goals. This is why choosing something you love is important. Be sure you're manifesting a goal that is truly yours!

To be honest with you, it took me many years to truly embrace the power and simplicity of this simple lesson – follow your passion and be yourself.

You manifest for yourself, not to impress others. Although, when you manifest your true goals, fame and recognition may manifest as a side effect of your main manifestation (if fame is what you want and you're ready for it!).

So, once again, choose your own goals. Do what feels good to you!

Once again, there's no judgment. From my experience, I can tell you that sometimes, it may take several attempts of trial and error just to see what you really want (especially if you're like me, and your ego is very, very talented and always wants to have the final say!).

Before we get into our energetic secrets to help you become a vibrational match to your desires, let's discuss what to avoid. In other words, how not to do this vibrational work...

And once again, the concept of alignment and authenticity of your goals and motivations comes up... One of the biggest hurdles so many people face when manifesting is getting in alignment with their true desires. And without alignment, there's no magic. You can achieve something by extreme sacrifice and hustle, only to end up burned out or unhappy.

I've been there too, and I tried hard to prove to others how great I was...

But deep inside, I didn't feel so great...

Finally, the pain of not living my life on my own terms and manifesting the same negative patterns all over again motivated me to dive deep and self-reflect on my beliefs, motivations, and authentic desires...

Looking back at my life, I'm grateful for everything I've experienced on my journey because now, I can turn my experiences into valuable manifesting lessons.

We don't fail, we succeed, or we learn!

The initial setbacks I experienced on my journey motivated me to become my own manifestation detective. I got curious about analyzing different patterns in my life to see when I was or wasn't in alignment.

Whenever I lacked alignment, I couldn't manifest what I wanted; or I didn't feel fulfilled when I did. Or, even if I could manifest what I wanted, for example, a new job, or client, something would always happen, and I would lose it.

So, once again, I put my LOA detective hat on and came to a very straightforward conclusion:

To become a vibrational match to your desires, aside from manifesting from pure, authentic energy, you need to:

1. Believe you can have what you want.
2. Give yourself the experience of feeling your desire in the present moment.

Now, it sounds simple on the surface...

And it is simple, but in the beginning, it may not be easy because we may need to take an honest look at our beliefs and what might be holding us back from fully believing in ourselves.

Now, when we dive deeper into the simple yet powerful teachings of *believe and feel it now*, it also makes sense to practice:

1. Mindfulness and living in the present moment- when you're fully present and embrace the here, and now, you experience incredible joy and harmony. At the same time, you separate yourself from worry, anxiety, and doubt; we already know these are the most significant manifestation killers.

It's hard to believe in something if, at the same time, you doubt it, right?

And how can you be a vibrational match to, let's say, manifesting a new house if you simultaneously doubt yourself or keep telling yourself and your friends how hard it is and how expensive everything gets?

Mindfulness and conscious manifesting go hand in hand. So, take a few small breaks during the day to take a few deep breaths and embrace the present moment. Remind yourself that you're safe, happy, loved, and abundant. Because you are! You live to experience unlimited joy.

At the same time, when you embrace the present moment, you go beyond the shackles of linear time. Embracing the present moment heals every moment of your life...

You stop feeling guilty about the past or worrying about the future. Instead, you embrace the present moment, where all possibilities exist.

And I'll repeat it; in fact, I urge you to turn it into your mantra or write it in your journal:

The Present Moment Heals!

2. The Gift of Conscious Heart-Based Meditation

When you take a few deep breaths and focus on the area of your heart, you realize that...you're always safe!

Your heart is harmony, love, peace, and joy.

My personal belief is that our hearts are manifestation magnets that connect us to the Divine Forces or whatever Higher Power or entity you believe in...

Your heart is where your Higher Self resides. And your Higher Self is always a vibrational match to the best things life has to offer...

Oh, and your Higher Self always knows what's good for you. It always makes good decisions...

So, whenever you're feeling stuck, or your mind loses its discipline and starts bombarding you with negative emotions of fear, doubt, or envy...let it go on a break.

And instead, focus on your heart...

Because when you're in your heart, you're automatically centered, peaceful, joyful, and full of love- and you give yourself the gift of the highest vibrations, automatically getting into the best vibrational match for all the good stuff in your life.

Now, here's the best part, even if you don't know what you want, or you realized that what you thought you wanted was very ego-based and not your goal, and now you're feeling confused or are looking for a new, exciting purpose or desire, your heart always knows what's good for you.

Your heart is the divine part of you. It's a divine messenger inside you. So, by allowing yourself to be more heart-centered while releasing negative emotions from your over-worried and overstressed mind, you get closer to the positive manifestations you desire and deserve.

Even if you don't know what they are...

Yes! By embracing the power of your heart, you can simply trust that you're manifesting something unique and unexpected, and you will become a vibrational match to it!

Why am I mentioning these two simple tips before getting into the main content of this book?

Well, because it can raise your vibration and compellingly shift your consciousness, even before we get into the nitty-gritty of vibrational alignment work.

Yes, what we're doing now is just a little aperitif...

The best is yet to come! For now, we're just hanging out together in this fantastic manifestation restaurant.

Also, some of the concepts I mention later in this book may require you to go deeper into your mindset and beliefs. And, from my personal experience, I know that sometimes, diving deeper may make us feel a bit uncomfortable, right?

And then we think: *hold on, that doesn't feel good, let's just skip it...*

Now, yes, I'm all about feeling good. But, working on your manifestation muscle requires work and effort, especially in the beginning.

It's not my intention to make you feel bad or uncomfortable. This is why I've just given you two very easy-to-apply techniques you can do whenever you want to embrace good feelings.

I often do heart-based meditation or embrace the present moment as I go deeper into my limiting beliefs or old mindsets.

And so, going deeper no longer makes me feel inadequate or uncomfortable!

It's like going to the gym and experiencing a bit of discomfort and pain (in a healthy and balanced way, of course, we don't want to experience any injuries) and then getting a nice massage...

The two techniques that precede the main part of this book are like a massage for your new, manifesting, and vibrational match muscles! And you can use them whenever you want, they are free and will always make you feel good. The more you practice them, the better!

You can also set an intention to be a vibrational match to inner work and manifestation secrets that make you feel good and always work for you while helping you transform.

You decide. And you get to choose the mindset that allows you to get the best out of this book. Yes, it's short. But it's meant to be read more than once. Because every time you read it, you'll be on a higher vibrational and consciousness level!

I'm doing this work continuously. I work on my alignment every day. The more I do it, the easier and more magical it gets.

I urge you to pick a goal you're passionate about and use this book to manifest it with joy and ease...

Even if, right now, you're not sure how you will ever manifest your goal, remember that all you need is to get started.

By getting started, you're showing the Universe that you're ready to receive guidance and are invested in manifesting your goal!

Have trust in yourself and be willing to take the next step. Keep moving in the direction of your goal. Stay calm and confident.

For example, I'm now becoming a vibrational match to writing this book. Even though I'm merely writing its introduction and don't know exactly how the rest will unfold, this book is already a future memory.

I have a strong intention as to what I desire to share and how I want to make my readers feel. My focus is on helping my readers soothe their inner states so that they can feel good and manifest whatever they desire with joy and ease! That's my alignment for writing.

This book is a fruit of my energetic alignment. It's done, and it's created. It has its own unique script. I know it's already finished, published, and successfully used by my beloved readers. Everything starts with energy!

All I need to do is to show up with authentic confidence and do my best by taking the next step. I trust myself and the Universe. The memory is already created. It exists in the quantum field of all possibilities.

Now, I show up for this book and my beautiful readers the best I can, from my best energies. I work on my mindset daily. And, in my mind, this book is already done and helping people.

Whatever it is I do or wish to pursue- I approach it from the same mindset...the Future Memory Mindset!

But it wasn't always like that. Before discovering this work, I could never get any creative project done. I was a prisoner of my mind, ego, and negative thoughts. I didn't trust myself. Instead, I stayed focused on multiple reasons why I couldn't do something...

Until one day, I discovered, or better said, re-discovered (because I already knew about it, it's that I didn't practice it, haha) the power of the lesson: *what you focus on expands...*

And I decided to apply some mindful mental discipline to...use the *what you focus on expands* principle in a positive way to become a vibrational match to what I wanted to manifest, not to what I wanted to avoid.

Now, it's my desire that you, too, apply these magical teachings to create a life you love and deserve!

Let's do this!

Secret #1 Audit Your Deep-Rooted Beliefs

Auditing your beliefs is a continuous process and a journey, especially if you're into unlimited growth and expansion. What blocks so many people from manifesting their desires is that they never look honestly at what may be blocking their manifestations. The reason? It may feel a bit uncomfortable at first.

I know it was for me! And, as I keep unpeeling some old layers of limiting beliefs, sometimes, I still feel a bit uncomfortable.

Luckily, we both know we can quickly embrace the power of the present moment and remind ourselves that we're safe and loved!

So, how can our beliefs block our manifestations?

Let's take money as an example. You can consciously set a goal to make a certain amount of money per month.

On the surface, it looks like you've done your homework, at least the logical part of it. For example, you know what kind of house you desire to own and how much it costs, and you calculate how much money you might need to be eligible for a good mortgage deal.

By staying focused on your goal, you activate your RAS (Reticular Activating System), remain focused on your goal, and manifest a new job or business opportunity or even some unexpected money.

But, if you still have some subconscious money blocks, for example, you can't hold onto money for a long time, or you get triggered when you hear someone is making more money than you do, or deep inside, you still feel you're not enough, you may self-sabotage your success.

So, if you want to reach the proper alignment and become a vibrational match to money so that you can always manifest more of it, whenever you need, you need to look at your limiting money stories and start to reverse them.

Now, my guess is that as children, most of us heard at least one of the following from our well-meaning parents and care-takers:

-*"Money can't buy us happiness."*

-*"I'd rather be happy than rich."*

-*"Money is the root of all evil."*

And, we probably found ourselves mindlessly repeating at least one of them (if not all). Unless we had parents or someone in our family who knew how to practice LOA for money and abundance...

Now, the purpose of going deeper is not to make you feel bad or cultivate resentment towards your loved ones. One thing I learned from Louise Hay (this mindset alone is very healing and helps raise your vibration while stepping into peaceful forgiveness) is that people always do the best they can with what they know based on their level of awareness. (I'm paraphrasing here).

Let me repeat:

People always do their best with what they know based on their level of awareness.

So, no judgment here!

When I started doing this work, I'd waste lots of time either beating myself up for some past decisions based on my old mindsets or even blaming my family for my lack of success.

I was the Queen of Self-Imposed Guilt-Trips. Not only that, but I also made many family members feel bad by judging their way of being and choices. I was new to self-development and was doing a little "crusade," trying to convert others to my way of living (it never works!).

I'd spent days or even months repeatedly thinking about and replaying what some family members did to me or said about me...

But here's the thing: the past is done!

Now, while doing some ancestral healing and understanding negative family patterns is helpful and healing, dwelling on our past is not!

Our true manifesting power lies right here in the present moment and gratitude. Whatever happens to you right now, you can transmute it into something positive, automatically healing your past.

All you need to do is to stay mindful of your thoughts. Ask yourself if a given thought or belief is helpful. Then, transform it into something more positive, healing all the past traumas and situations associated with this old belief.

Needless to say, blaming others and staying in a vibration of resentment is definitely not the key to becoming a vibrational match to our desires unless, for some reason, we desire to torment ourselves with negative, self-imposed feelings.

Once again, if you ever find yourself in such a mindset, embrace the power of the present moment and bathe in the joys and goodness of your heart.

After experimenting with different approaches to releasing our limitations, I realized that we don't always need to know where our beliefs came from. The main focus is to simply let them go while raising our vibration.

Our power is always in the present moment.

So, let's say you discover you feel a bit jealous or resentful when you see someone more successful than you. Or perhaps, there's a goal you've been working on, and someone achieves something similar faster?

This has happened to me recently! Someone I know achieved what I'm working on right now.

I began thinking about that person and how everyone praised them and their achievements. I caught myself in self-defeating thoughts: "Why is this taking so long? Why do other people always succeed so smoothly, and for me, it seems to take ages? Or maybe, they did something unethical, which is why they're so successful?"

And I immediately knew I was lowering my vibration and had to stop.

I knew it was all coming from a limiting belief: "I must be doing something wrong."

Not very empowering...and certainly not helping anyone in their right senses be a vibrational match to something amazing!

Remember – *what we focus on expands!*

Now, back to my limiting beliefs around money and achievement…I didn't really go deep down into my childhood but asked myself: "Is this really true? Will I allow it to be my truth? How can I transform it into my new, empowering truth?".

And I replaced it with a new, empowering belief such as:

"I'm exactly where I need to be. Everything is unfolding as it should. Seeing other people succeed makes me believe in myself even more!".

I also said to myself:

"Elena, you're not here to judge. Release the need to judge others and how fast or slow they should achieve success; release the need to compare yourself."

Getting on the vibration of no judgment and no comparison, where everything just is, and there are no levels, is a gift in itself (and a wonderful manifestation of a higher level of awareness!).

Then, instead of staying in the negative vibration of comparison and envy, I decided to bless that person and their achievements. I thought to myself: "Wow, the

Universe sent me this person as a signal to let me know that I, too, can manifest my personal goals. I'm on the right path. Everything is possible!".

Here are several questions that can help you shift your thoughts to more empowering ones:

-Is this really true?

-Is holding onto this belief worth it? Why not change it and manifest what I want faster?

-Will this thought or issue even matter in 5 years from now?

-What about my new self? My new self already lives in our dream reality. What are her thoughts?

So, the most important takeaway from this secret is to keep auditing your thoughts and beliefs. If manifesting money is your desire, how do you react to wealthy people, their habits, and what they do with their money? How do you feel when someone shares their success stories?

If you realize you're feeling envious, don't worry, don't beat yourself up. Be grateful that now you're aware of it. Then, slowly, start using your mind positively and think beautiful and empowering thoughts that align with your desires.

For example, you may feel triggered that someone who seems to be working way less than you do, got their dream home. And they paid it off already.

Your brain might even tell you: "Oh, they probably did something dishonest!".

Luckily, now you know how it works and so you are in total control of your thoughts.

Ask yourself: "Is this thought taking me closer to my desired manifestations or taking away from them?"

Then, release the need to judge. Instead, focus your precious energy on changing your thoughts and actions toward your goal.

Instead of feeling envy, you can feel a sense of inspiration. The Universe is showing you that abundance exists. And you, too, can tune into it by changing your vibrational frequency.

Another question you can ask yourself to shift out of your old, limiting thoughts is:

"But what if…"

For example: *"But what if, right now, I could manifest my dream home…how would I feel?"*.

Or: *"But what if there was some new, unexpected way to manifest my desires faster?"*.

Now, you're on a new, more empowering vibration. The vibration of more possibilities. You can take it one step further and embrace the vibration of limitless quantum possibilities.

Finally, use the Law of Assumption and tell yourself a better story, for example:

"Why am I wasting my time on these old, disempowering thoughts? I already have my dream house. I'm living in it and having the time of my life. I believe everyone deserves to manifest their desires. I am so happy for myself and others. I love living in abundance, and seeing others live in abundance fills my heart with joy. Thank You - Thank You - Thank You!".

This is the power of positive transformation. Our old, limiting beliefs can be used to help us shift to a more empowering vibration and become a match for what we desire! I see limiting beliefs and triggers as our best inner healers. As I mentioned several times in my previous books: *triggers are healers!*

Same with limiting beliefs. They can be quickly shifted to new, empowering beliefs.

If the Universe makes you see someone abundant, it's because they allow you to feel their joy and get on a higher vibration. Why waste it on thinking negative and limiting thoughts of envy, jealousy, and victim mindset?

You're a victor, and you can have *anything* you want.

Focus on your vibration and take good care of it. It will set you free and help you manifest your desires with joy and ease.

And yes, from my experience, you don't always need to know precisely where your limiting beliefs came from. Yes, it may be helpful and healing.

However, you may also use this approach- simply transform your limiting beliefs into new, empowering ones while raising your vibration and feeling grateful for everything the Universe sends you.

You determine your inner state! So, you can discover you have a limiting belief and quickly release it or transform it into something positive without exactly knowing where it came from.

Practice it starting today! Start auditing and shifting your thoughts. Be mindful of how you react to other people's success and achievements.

Release the need to compete or compare yourself with others. Follow your path and be mindful of your vibration!

Secret #2 Activate Your Inner Leadership

It's done, my dear. You have your desire. You have manifested it. So...what are your thoughts and behaviors now that you have manifested your goals?

The exercise we're going to practice in this chapter is very simple. Its main aim is to help you become a vibrational match to your desires and preferred outcomes by *being* it!

Modern psychology and self-development literature often refer to this concept as self-image. And since we're doing all this work to fuse ourselves with our desires and be one with them, feel good about them right here and right now – it's all about creating your new, empowered self-image.

I'm very passionate about doing self-image work (something I incorporate into my inner work daily). I'm very consistent with my self-image message throughout all my books and articles.

I know self-image works, and it's an extremely powerful concept. But, I've observed, both from my own experience and by sharing this powerful concept with others, that the primary reason people fail with it is that they do it once or twice and forget about it. Or they get scared of their new self and reverse back to the old. Some are still vibrating in a negative way by worrying about: "What will others think?"

*(please let Elena liberate you from this mindset, and limiting vibration, right here, right now – it's not about what others think, it's about what **you** think – after all, you create your reality with your thoughts, not someone else's thoughts, right?).*

Of course, it's not my intention to judge anyone or make them feel bad. I also experienced the negative vibrations of reverting back to my old self. But I promised myself to figure it out and turn my negative experiences into something positive that could help others.

Sometimes I look back at my life and experience some self-defeating, guilty thoughts about what I should have done or how my life could have been if only this and that or if I'd been born into a different family.

These are all ego-based thoughts and are not helping us with anything at all. They are only taking us away from our vibrational and manifesting alignment work.

I love to give a positive meaning to everything that happens in my life. I apply this mindset to my inner work and spiritual growth journey. As I told you, I also experienced some setbacks due to reversing back into my old patterns. However, since I'm fully immersed in this work, I can catch myself falling off track and correct my path. Whereas, before doing my inner work, I'd flow unconsciously in the ocean of negativity and resentment.

Also, I immediately think about my beautiful readers and the people I desire to help and guide. I ask myself- how can I turn this negative experience and unconscious fall back into something positive? And so, I always manage to find a way to use it to convey some positive lessons or teachings.

That way, I turn everything that happens in my life into a positive experience and lesson for myself and others! Why not let others learn from our mistakes so that they can avoid them and grow faster? At least we give our past mistakes a meaning...that alone is a potent vibration booster, right?

So, why am I telling you this? Why can't I just give you a technique to do now and hope you do well?

Well, techniques are great, but they must be a part of something bigger, a more aligned system or a principle that leads us in a particular direction.

Our main direction here is to raise our vibration to be a match for the good stuff in our lives and attract amazing things the heart-based way, or, in case you desire to attract something more specific, be a match for that.

And I'm just about to share a compelling self-image work technique. But here's one thing to understand:

I know that self-image work may also have its traps. Don't get me wrong, it's very effective.

But only if you commit to it. I, too, used to be guilty of doing it halfway and reversing back to my old self, then blaming myself and others and therefore getting back into my old, negative vibrations.

I don't want this to happen to you!

Therefore, before immersing yourself in a technique from this chapter, I want you to understand these two concepts:

#1 You need to unleash your inner leadership!

You can take it one step further and declare that you're your own leader.

Now, the work I share in this chapter is often labeled as self-image, self-concept, etc., as this is how all self-help and spirituality books refer to it.

But what really works for me, vibrationally, is truly internalizing this work and referring to it as activating your inner leader.

So, how does it feel to be your own leader?

To me, it feels great! It feels authentically powerful. But with that power also comes great responsibility. You and only you are responsible for doing your inner work.

Yes, many books and mentors can help you and guide you. But the true and only power is in your hands.

Don't throw it away. Use it to your advantage!

As a self-leader, you show up for yourself and lead yourself daily. You are responsible for your vibration and doing your inner work.

You are responsible for your results. No more blame. You can't blame others, and you can't blame yourself either. There's no such thing as blame and judgment for you now. Because now, you are fully resourceful and create your own way! Stick to it and keep going.

Say this with me: *I am the leader of my own reality. I now unleash my inner leadership!*

#2 See yourself as someone who leads others

Even if you're not in any leadership position professionally, and even if you don't have children and don't take care of anyone, and don't lead anyone, please do yourself a favor and see yourself as someone who leads and inspires others.

See yourself as a spiritual teacher. Even if you're not a spiritual teacher of any kind and have no desire to be one, even if you're not a light worker and even if you're very new to reading books like this one, see yourself as a leader.

Because you are a leader. The leader. The leader of light and truth. Love and the highest and purest vibrations.

So, whatever happens in your life...if you ever reverse back to your old self, turn it into your own teaching and imagine you share it with others to empower them.

Remember- there's no guilt, blame, or judgment, so there's no more space to indulge in negativity.

This is what I do! My life's purpose as a light worker turned writer is to turn negative into positive and share everything I've learned with others to make their journeys as smooth as possible. But since I understand that their most considerable growth will come from integrating my teachings into their own lives in their unique way, I always intend to raise their level of awareness. Because if you can think highly vibrational thoughts, you will attract highly vibrational people and circumstances into your life.

The main reason people come back to my books is not because I'm the greatest writer in the world but because I always intend to integrate my highest vibrations and make my readers experience high frequencies in their own unique way, no matter their circumstances. But this is a topic for another day!

So, to recap, you're just about to learn a new technique. I call it Unleash Your Inner Leadership, but the concept itself is based around self-image or self-concept work, and it's one of the main pillars of almost all self-help and spirituality books aimed at facilitating transformation.

The principles you need to integrate into your life to make the Unleash Your Inner Leadership exercise make work for you are:

-Be your own leader- you are the leader of your own reality, so release the judgment, blaming others or yourself. It doesn't exist in our reality. No more floating unconsciously in the ocean of blame!

-See yourself as someone who leads others by turning whatever happens to you into some spiritual teaching you could share with others to help them.

Now you're ready to practice some of the most powerful vibrational techniques.

Most people get stuck in the energy of wanting to manifest something, and all they think about is what they want. Now, there's nothing wrong with this approach, and many LOA and self-development books tell you to stay focused on what you want, right?

But sometimes, these teachings are not complete or not interpreted correctly.

Because, to make it work fully, you need to understand that there are two components to it. There's what you desire and who you are.

What you want + who you are = full vibrational match!

For example, a person could think about money and expensive mansions all day. But if they don't think like wealthy people do and can't handle their money wisely, all they will achieve is wishful thinking, not a conscious manifestation. Or even if they manifest, they might lose it all.

First, you think about your genuine, heart-based desire that makes you feel good.

And then, you ask yourself: *OK, so who am I right now and who do I need to become to fuse myself with my desires?*

How do I act? What do I think?

People in healthy relationships tend to think happy and healthy thoughts about themselves and their loved ones. They radiate positive emotions of unconditional love.

That isn't to say that they don't experience occasional bad days or little disagreements with their loved ones.

But…even if they do, they can quickly shift out of these misalignments and return to their love-based default state.

People who manifest large amounts of money have specific thoughts about money. They don't waste their time or energy resenting others for having money or judging other people's jobs or businesses.

As someone who was able to make a significant vibrational jump in the area of manifesting money, I can tell you this: the old me would block her money flow by constantly feeling resentment towards people with money and thinking thoughts such as:

"Oh, they are probably from a rich family."

"Oh, they just got lucky."

"Oh, they are probably not very ethical."

It took me some effort to create a new, abundant version of myself with new thoughts and belief systems.

And you can do this for any area of life you desire to manifest success in. It works for money, love, and health.

Talking about health and fitness, I also had many limiting beliefs in this area, and I would resent people for having a good workout routine or a clean and healthy diet plan. The old me would even bully them.

Oh, their lives must be so dull!

Not very healthy thoughts to think! And definitely not very empowering to stay inspired to take care of yourself.

So, here's your homework...

You need a piece of paper divided into 2 parts.

You can also use 2 pieces of paper or a journal.

This exercise aims to help you see your old and new selves clearly.

Under your old self, you want to write down all the old, limiting beliefs that are blocking your manifestations.

For example:

-uncomfortable when seeing other people succeed;

-jealous of other people's success in business or their area of expertise;

-too scared to look at your bank account balance;

-feeling guilty, scared or angry when paying for something.

Oh, and don't worry about writing down your old limiting beliefs. Now that you're conscious of them, they have no power over you. So, writing them down will not amplify them or turn them into unwanted manifestations.

But you will be aware when your old self knocks on your door, and you'll be able to kindly let them go or even fully retire.

Our focus now is on creating your new self!

In alignment with that, you want to create your new self-concept and be conscious of your new, empowering thoughts, beliefs, actions, and habits.

For example: Your New Self

-happy and inspired when seeing other people succeed;

-fully present, grateful, and living in the present moment;

-accepts people as they are and releases all the judgment;

-feels confident about money and loves learning about the best ways to handle large amounts of money;

-understands that money is abundant, chooses to feel happy and grateful when spending money, knowing that money is a renewable resource and always flows back!

Now, you don't just do this exercise once. You create your list of limiting and empowering beliefs and look at those beliefs every day, preferably in the morning. Of course, your focus is on your new self!

Every morning, promise to fuse yourself with your new self as much as possible. Simply do your best! Be self-compassionate about this process.

Focus on gradually embodying your new self every day. Remember that every day and every situation you experience is an opportunity for you to practice your new self-image. Also, remember that everything in your life is a spiritual lesson.

Release any need to be perfect at this from day one!

The main feature of our Universe is that of infinity. There's no beginning and no end. So, you're growing and expanding. You're constantly transforming yourself.

Your focus is on mindfully becoming your new self while embracing self-compassion and self-awareness. Take a mental screenshot of your list, and as you go throughout your day, play a game with it!

Keep asking yourself: *"Hmm, what would the new self do in this situation? How would she think?"*

At the same time, don't feel bad about your old self, beliefs, and thoughts. Remember, you were doing the best you could based on your level of awareness back then.

But now, your awareness is shifting, and you're becoming a vibrational match to your desires. Don't fall asleep. Cultivate your new levels of understanding.

Yes, some mental effort and discipline are required in the beginning. But eventually, playing the game of your inner leadership will become automatic, joyful, and fun.

Be a good, compassionate, heart-based yet demanding self-leader. Set clear rules for yourself and stick to them. It's your life and your rules. You can be, do, and have whatever you desire. Nobody has any right to judge you, and you can allow yourself to be your new self!

Whenever you catch yourself thinking some old, limiting, or negative thoughts, ask yourself:

"Is this really true? Is this like a Universal law or something?".

Well, probably it's just your old self knocking on your door. Once again, they can retire now! They did what they could with what they knew. Their old thoughts and limiting beliefs might have even been good for you at some stage of your life. They were meant to protect you.

But now, it's the time for you to shine. So, focus on your new self.

If your old thoughts get too heavy or too negative, ask yourself:

Is it really worth it? How do these negative thoughts affect my vibration?

Short answer: *It's not worth it...*

My positive vibration is the most important thing in my life. I don't have any more time and energy to waste on my old, limiting thoughts. Instead, I choose to think positive thoughts of abundance and think about the things I like while becoming my new self.

Example:

Old limiting thought:

"I'm not good enough or smart enough to achieve my goals...."

Question your old thought:

Is this really true? Is it a law or something?

The short answer is- it's not true!

And you can choose to entertain a better thought such as: "What would be the first step to get closer to my dreams?"

You could spend more time in meditation or prayer to ask for guidance from the spiritual realm.

You could also find a mentor who could guide you.

In other words, by eliminating your old vibrations created by your old thoughts and consciously focusing on what you want, by becoming what you want and thinking thoughts that align with your desires, you become proactive.

Now, you can use your creative energy to manifest solutions for the next stage of your journey!

Have you noticed how you can align your new thoughts with new, empowering actions? For example, you install a new positive belief that you can master your craft, start a business, or succeed in your chosen field. Since you believe you can, you decide to hire a mentor or sign up for a professional course you need to embark on a new career. You also take spiritual actions. For example, you meditate or pray and ask for guidance, especially for the next step of your journey. You know what you desire, and you know who you are!

Because when you think as your new self, taking action begins to feel joyful and fun!

So, spend some time in self-reflection. How does it feel to operate from a new level of awareness and play the game of your inner leadership?

Many people experience peace and harmony. Whenever I dive deep into my inner leadership, I embrace the feeling of knowing that I will succeed. I release all stress, anxiety, and doubt. I immediately envision my new self and release any notions of linear time. I am my future memory. It's here and now. And it's always been. I know I'm on the right track, and the process is a beautiful destination. There's no more wanting, longing, or needing.

Whenever I activate my inner leader, I feel an amazing sense of purpose, clarity, and inner peace.

And these feelings are conducive to smooth and effective manifesting! For now, allow yourself to spend some time with your inner leader. In the next chapter, we will focus on feelings that will help you to vibrate even higher!

Secret #3 The Power of Letting Go and LOA Detox (Feel Good Just to Feel Good)

It took me years of exploration and experimentation to discover this little secret and use it to manifest many amazing things into my life.

But before I reveal it to you, let me ask you this question: as someone who is into the Law of Attraction, manifestation, and spirituality, have you ever felt overwhelmed with everything you *should* do around your desires?

You know…feel good about your desires, visualize your desires, and affirm your desires. Don't get me wrong, I'm all for doing all these techniques…but from a place of alignment and feeling good…

So, my question is: have you ever found yourself feeling overwhelmed or even psyched out about your desires, how long it took to manifest them, how much information you could consume, and what not?

Because I have felt that way...constantly feeling scared of making a mistake or manifesting something terrible. Or perhaps, not sticking to my manifestation practices long enough and not attracting my desires.

After talking to hundreds of people who practice manifestation with great success, I realized that most of them felt exactly like I did (feeling obsessed about this manifesting thing, but not in a good way). And being too obsessed with something and desperately trying to attract it can only slow us down.

This happens when we try to practice manifestation strictly from our logical minds because our over-analytical minds love to play tricks on us! They love to stay active, so they often try to "bless" us with doubt, non-stop negative chatter, and other not-so-pleasant feelings.

And that simple conclusion led me to do a little experiment. I decided to go on a little LOA detox and let go of my desires. Instead, I decided to focus on self-care and things I enjoyed doing. In other words, I decided to live my life and fully accepted myself exactly like I was.

Back then, I was pretty new to manifestation and didn't really understand the power of letting go. Nowadays, there's much more information available about the power of letting go. This concept is often discussed in LOA communities as a part of a successful and joyful manifestation process.

Because when we try too hard to be a match for what we desire, we may start to experience a manifestation roller coaster. One moment we feel scared and negative. Then, we try to be super positive. We keep jumping from one state to another, in a very extreme way. That often slows down our progress and reverberates on our mental health.

So, I decided to do a little experiment and was utterly detached from my desires. Instead, I filled my free time with activities that made me feel good. So, in a way, I decided to feel good, just to feel good.

This may seem very counterintuitive to some people. But trust me when I say this – *it always works!*

I still scripted, visualized, and affirmed as I continued my little manifesting detox.

But not about any of my desires!

Instead, I used visualization to think about good memories from my life. I kept replaying all the beautiful moments and focused on the good things in my life.

I didn't have to use my mental and creative energies to forcefully conjure up specific visualizations related to my desires that insisted on a particular scenario to try to attract something. Instead, I decided to go freestyle and visualized myself doing the things I loved. In my visualizations, I focused on happy memories. So, my mind got busy with positive stuff and didn't have much space for worry or doubt.

It felt like shifting to a neutral, peaceful state where all my needs were met. I'd still attend my old job and do my daily chores. But something inside me had changed. I went to my job feeling passionate, joyful, and fulfilled. Even though the job I had back then wasn't my passion and wasn't well-paid either, in my mind, I visualized myself being highly successful, using the power of the present moment, and feeling good).

I decided to return to yoga and signed up for yoga classes. Yoga has been a massive passion of mine ever since I was a teenager, but, at some stage, I stopped practicing it, because I felt like I had to use all my energy on making a living, studying manifestation, and trying hard to manifest a new job using the Law of Attraction.

Once again...when we try too hard, with too much-forced negativity, it may have the opposite effect, and we're definitely not in vibrational alignment. I'm sure you understand it by now.

Joining yoga classes felt so good, and it helped me release anxiety and feel good in my body.

I also met many amazing people and would often get invited to mindfulness resorts and healthy food parties. I experienced many unforgettable spiritual moments.

I felt loved and well taken care of by my world. I picked up many new hobbies, such as hiking and creating healthy recipes. It felt so good! And it still does because now I use this memory to feel good and be a vibrational match to more good stuff in my life.

As for scripting, I stopped scripting about my desires for a while. Back then, I desired a well-paying job and spent months chasing different opportunities and "trying to manifest." I still did my daily journaling, but instead of trying to attract my desire and feeling psyched out about it, I decided to start a happy journal. I wrote about the things that made me feel good such as happy memories or daily gratitude.

I felt grateful for the little and big things in my life. My gratitude wasn't attached to what I wanted to manifest. My gratitude was unconditional!

I felt grateful for my old job because it allowed me to pay my rent, and bills, buy food and pay for yoga classes. But I also felt immense gratitude for other areas of my life, such as meeting new friends and improving my social skills, learning how to cook healthy food, and the spiritual experiences I had in my meditations.

So, without even trying, I slowly began manifesting some little goals and desires I'd had for years, such as feeling peaceful and having a healthy lifestyle and new friends who loved me for who I was. When I realized how much power I had, I felt so moved! Oh, and I felt thankful I decided to prioritize myself and my wellbeing (instead of getting caught up in chasing money and burning myself out).

That experience taught me the power of feeling good and how prioritizing our self-care, holistic wellbeing, passions, and hobbies can help us become powerful manifestors. I believe in the power of *relax to manifest!*

Oh, and I still used affirmations. But once again, not to try to attract my dream job, but to feel good about myself, my life, and the present moment. I'd look at myself in the mirror and affirmed how much I loved and appreciated myself and how smart and resilient I was.

So, I used all the Law of Attraction techniques, such as journaling, affirmations, and visualizations, but to let go, be in the present moment, and feel good, just to feel good and appreciate my efforts.

After doing my *feel good, let go, and being in the present moment* protocols, I manifested a new job with no stress at all. It felt like that job found me because one of my yoga buddies recommended my CV to a company he worked for.

That experience taught me the importance of choosing myself and following my little passions and desires in the present moment. Don't postpone your wellbeing. Don't wait until you manifest your dream job, new house, or more money. Feel good now! You can let go to manifest! If you dive deeper into this concept and do a little research, you'll find many more people who began manifesting just by letting go!

Oh, but some may say: "Hold on...aren't we supposed to be persistent?"

Yes, but that depends on what being persistent means.

If one's interpretation of being persistent means burning oneself out, or sacrificing wellbeing in one area of life for something else, then, for me, it's not worth it.

But, if staying persistent means having a pure desire to find an effective, heart-based manifesting system that works for you and knowing when to slow down and when to speed up, in other words, understanding your own rhythm and cycle, then, of course, I'm a big proponent of that!

Stay persistent, hold your vision and live in balance while appreciating the present moment! We've heard it so many times, right? Our hearts know and understand this message, but our scattered minds often forget it.

For example, joining yoga classes was not connected to a higher-paying, more fulfilling job I wanted to manifest back then. But it felt good at a time. I felt guided to join yoga classes and reconnect with my old passion.

Instead of staying at home and getting psyched out about trying to attract a new job and feel good about it (while experiencing a manifestation roller coaster), I decided to focus on embracing the present moment.

And so, feeling good and being in the present moment became my default state. I was already feeling whole and complete with what I had. This is why I automatically became a vibrational match to what I desired back then.

Now, I no longer call such practices a manifestation detox because they had become a part of my lifestyle and what I do. It's not a manifestation detox nor a manifestation diet. It's just something I do. I like to relax, just to relax, and feel good just to feel good.

That's the true power of letting go!

It's hard to describe it in words, so I urge you to try it! Pick at least one passion or hobby you love. It doesn't have to connect to your desire (just like in my case, joining yoga classes didn't connect to manifesting a new, better-paying job).

The Universe wants you to feel good just because you deserve to feel good. And it already knows your desires. So, you don't have to constantly recite or affirm what you want. Instead, let go, and focus on feeling good.

If you receive any inspiration or guidance, act on it. But, in the meantime, think about the things that make you feel good. Start a gratitude journal. Visualize and replay good moments from your life! Use affirmations to talk to yourself kindly and embrace the power of the present moment.

As you embrace the feelings of wholeness and happiness, right here and now, you'll be a vibrational match to anything you want in your life, without even trying!

That doesn't mean you're not allowed to think about your desires. If you feel like it, then go for it!

From my experience, whenever I'm fully immersed in feel-good rituals and the present moment, and I am inspired to think about my desires, they feel so real to me that I find myself saying: "Thank You - Thank You - Thank You" to the Universe, almost automatically.

Test it for yourself! So many people experience amazing manifestations just by letting go.

Also, this book's previous steps and secrets serve as tools to help you release your limiting beliefs and think in a new, empowering way. By letting go of what no longer serves you, you automatically vibrate higher and higher, unleashing the power of effortless or magical manifestations!

Conclusion – A Few More Vibrational Tricks to Boost Your Manifesting Powers

Now, it's time to put everything you've learned so far into practice! This book is short for a reason. While I'm confident that reading this book alone can help you raise your vibration and feel good, you'll get the best results by using these teachings in your daily life.

Remember what we said at the beginning of this book? Your life is your best teacher, and you have the power to turn every obstacle into a fantastic opportunity.

I finished writing this book a week ago, and then I went on a little holiday to see my family. As I mentioned, I wanted this book to be short – 3 chapters with 3 secrets that are easy to apply and can bring joy and success to my readers' lives.

But, as I got back home, more inspiration manifested, and so I decided to enrich this book with a few more vibrational tips so that we conclude our journey with something practical and powerful.

They are a quick way to shift out of any negative situation and instantly raise your vibration. However, you can also incorporate them into your daily manifesting practice! Use your heart as a guide because your heart always knows!

Tip #1 Future Memories Gratitude Exercise

So...here's what happened. Not only did you manifest your desires....you actually surpassed them! Yes, you manifested all your desires and more! Now, it's time to express your gratitude.

Yes, it is done. You manifested your big dreams. So, how does it feel? Write about it using the following format:

I feel so happy and grateful that I manifested my desire because (and explain why you're grateful).

Explaining *why* you're feeling grateful for something is a very effective yet often overlooked vibrational booster.

For example:

-I feel so happy and grateful that I own my dream house and that it's all paid off because now, I don't have any more rent or mortgage payments, and it feels good to have this money for myself!

-*I feel so happy and grateful that I have my own beautiful house because now I have more space to invite my family and friends and have a fantastic time together.*

-*I feel so happy and grateful for my new house and that it's now mine, all paid for because now, I can paint and decorate it exactly the way I want!*

Or: *I feel so happy and grateful for my new, successful business. Finally, I can work from home, doing what I love. The money is so good. I can't believe I manifested such a high-paying opportunity! On top of that, my business is very flexible, so I can travel the world and spend more time with my family.*

Once again- the main trick here is adding *why* you're grateful for something because it helps you to energetically align with your desires even more! You're not just mindlessly stating why you're thankful for something. You're actually tapping into positive emotions and good feelings, and these are the best vibrational match secrets to live in alignment.

Tip#2 Meet a Friend - Vibrational Exercise

This exercise is a variation of the previous tip and is perfect for those not fond of scripting. It can be done in two different ways – live or imaginary.

For example, if you have a friend who's into manifesting, you can meet in person and share your gratitude for what you've manifested so far.

But...we release the linear concept of time. So, you can be grateful for anything...even things you can't see in your physical reality yet.

At the same time, congratulate your friend on their success. Celebrate! Turn your meeting into a fantastic celebration that feels good.

You can also do this exercise in your mind by visualizing yourself sharing your success with someone you love. Express your gratitude and tell your friend how happy you are now that you know how to use the Law of Attraction to your favor.

Tip#3 Normalize Your Desire

This tip can be applied to all areas of your life, but I found it helpful for manifesting money and abundance.

Why? For many people, money equals negative emotions (fear, envy, worry, jealousy, resentment).

All these negative emotions block the flow of abundance (or whatever you desire to manifest). This is why, if you want to become a vibrational match to money, you need to enter what I like to call a clean state, where you feel like money and abundance are absolutely normal.

So how to normalize money? It all starts with your thoughts. Your thoughts can bring you closer to or further away from your desire. Of course, if you're reading this book, I assume your goal is to manifest more of what you desire and with more ease, right?

Once again, I'm using money as an example here. However, this exercise can be used to normalize all your desires so that you fuse yourself with them instead of separating yourself from them and attracting more of a gap (that can feel like: "I guess this is not for me" or "Others can do it, I can't.")

To do this exercise, I'd recommend you start a "normalization" journal and internalize your new truths by talking to yourself in front of the mirror.

Step #1 Know that you are worthy simply because you exist. You don't need to prove anything to anyone!

Keep affirming and writing down affirmations such as: "It's absolutely normal for me to have a 6-figure job I love", "It's absolutely normal for me to enjoy different sources of passive income," or "It's absolutely normal for me to achieve even the so-called unrealistic goals".

(I mean...as a creator and leader of your reality, you decide what's real, and everything can be real and easy to manifest if you decide so!).

Step #2 Promise yourself to feel safe and comfortable around your desires.

For example, if you want to attract more money, keep journaling about how you spend and invest your money and how normal it feels to you to keep manifesting more income!

And whenever you feel guilty about spending money, focus on the value that the products or services you're buying provide you with. Bless the products and service creators you purchase from. Feel into their flow of abundance. How does it feel to be a part of it?

Step #3 Stay open and receptive to money.

Keep affirming:

"I am open to receiving more," and "I am ready to reach the next level of abundance."

At the same time, keep reminding yourself that you can trust yourself with money. You see, many people affirm that they are open and ready to receive more abundance. But they also subconsciously fear money and abundance because they are unsure if they can trust themselves with money.

This is why adding affirmations such as: "I feel supported by money," and "I can trust myself with money" is very helpful.

Keep affirming that you're very good at attracting, saving, and investing money and that you always find great professionals who help you make good money decisions.

In alignment with your affirmations and money energy work, whenever you see an opportunity to learn more about money management in alignment with your values, go for it! Money management is not the same as some scarcity budgeting. Of course, I am not bashing budgeting as such, because, if done with good energy it can actually help you feel grateful and abundant. All I am saying is that scarcity, fear and shame-based budgeting is not the best way to create abundance....

(This topic goes beyond the scope of this book, so, I'd recommend you check out my books: Money Mindset & Law of Attraction for Abundance to dive deeper into money vibes!).

Now, back to aligned money management to help you become a vibrational match to money...Such money management can be fascinating and fun, especially when you approach it from a higher vibration and access the feelings of limitless abundance and wealth.

Now, you may be aware that many spiritual people reject the concept of money management or learning about good money strategies and ways to make it, save it or invest it. Hence, so many people get put off it!

I used to be like that, and that mindset only pushed my abundance away. But, with a bit of work and guidance from both my spiritual teachers and financial advisors, I broke through my limiting beliefs around money and successfully combined spiritual work with practical work such as money management.

Attracting money is easier for me because I no longer block myself with old mindsets such as: "What if I make more money and someone takes it away?"

To sum up, one of the most important things to be a precise vibrational match to what you want is to form an identity as someone who already has what you desire and feels very comfortable with it. In fact, it's absolutely normal for them.

Back to the example of becoming a vibrational match to money, many people block themselves because they stay stuck in some old stories and guilt trips around past money mistakes or mindsets such as what other people think of them.

This has to go right here, right now. Remember that you're safe. You can always go within yourself and find peace, love, safety, and abundance. Now, as for "what will others think of me," let me liberate you from this limiting belief too. First of all, it doesn't matter what others think. *All that matters is what **YOU** think.* You create your reality with your own thoughts, not someone else's. Oh, and most people are stuck worrying about what others think of them, so it's not that they constantly think about you and your past mistakes...so that should give you some relief, right?

We've all made some money mistakes in the past, so what? Money can always be made and re-created. And it's all about learning from your mistakes. So, release all your old stories. Right here and right now.

Make the present moment your best friend.

The present moment heals you.

The present moment creates your new reality.

The present moment strengthens you.

The present moment helps you feel good.

And heart-based manifesting is all about feeling good!

Until the next time we meet, I wish you unlimited peace, love, abundance, and whatever it is you desire!

It's time to turn your life into true manifesting magic.

The power is in your hands!

Much love,

Elena

Your friend and guide in conscious manifesting

Join Our Manifestation Newsletter and Get a Free eBook

To help you amplify what you've learned in this book, I'd like to offer you a free copy of my LOA Workbook – a powerful, FREE 5-day program (eBook & audio) designed to help you raise your vibration while eliminating resistance and negativity.

To sign up for free, visit the link below now:

www.loaforsuccess.com/newsletter

You'll also get free access to my inspirational LOA Newsletter to help you stay high vibe!

Through this email newsletter, I regularly share all you need to know about the manifestation mindset and energy.

Plus, whenever I release a new book, you can get it at a deeply discounted price.

To sign up for free, visit the link below now:

www.loaforsuccess.com/newsletter

If you happen to have any technical issues with your sign-up, please email us at:

support@LOAforSuccess.com

Recommended Books by Elena G.Rivers – Now Available on Amazon

www.ingramcontent.com/pod-product-compliance
Lightning Source LLC
Chambersburg PA
CBHW072103110526
44590CB00018B/3297